THE
RONALD REAGAN

COLORING BOOK

ARTIST: MORT DRUCKER
WRITER: PAUL LAIKIN

Andrews and McMeel
A Universal Press Syndicate Company
Kansas City • New York

A COMPLETE LISTING OF
RONNIE'S ACCOMPLISHMENTS

DEDICATION
This book is dedicated to an administration
that would like to take us back
to the good old days. To 1929.

SPECIAL THANKS
to Barbara Drucker and Eden Laikin

The Ronald Reagan Coloring Book copyright © 1988 by Mort Drucker and Paul Laikin. All rights reserved. Printed in the United States of America. No part of this book may be used or reproduced in any manner without written permission except in the case of reprints in the context of reviews. For information write Andrews and McMeel, a Universal Press Syndicate Company, 4900 Main Street, Kansas City, Missouri 64112.

Library of Congress Catalog Card Number: 87-73261

ISBN: 0-8362-1826-4

This is our Ronnie.
Do not bother to color him.
It is a waste of time.
He is like Teflon.
Nothing will stick to him.
Ronnie did a lot for his country.
He will soon retire from public life.
That will be *another* good thing he'll do for his country.

This is our Nancy.
Isn't she elegant looking?
Color her royal blue.
Nancy is always at her Ronnie's side.
He never makes a move without her.
You always see her whispering in his ear.
She tells him what to say and what to do.
It is *Nancy* who is running the country!

These were two of Ronnie's closest advisers.
They were always fighting with each other.
Color them black and blue.
Ronnie could never control his advisers.
Don't you find this very puzzling?
If he couldn't stop his own *staff* from fighting—
how did he expect to stop the fighting
in the Middle East?

Color this man important.
He is Ronnie's second-in-command.
This man ran with our Ronnie.
He is still running today.
He doesn't know when to stop.
A lot of people do not like this man.
We can't understand why, can you?
After all, he hasn't *done* anything!

See Ronnie and Nancy walking to their helicopter?
They are going to their ranch in California.
It is another of their many vacations.
Color them tan and in the pink.
See Ronnie trying to answer a reporter's question?
The helicopter is so noisy he can't hear a thing.
That's why Ronnie likes to be asked questions there.
If he can't hear 'em, he can't answer 'em!

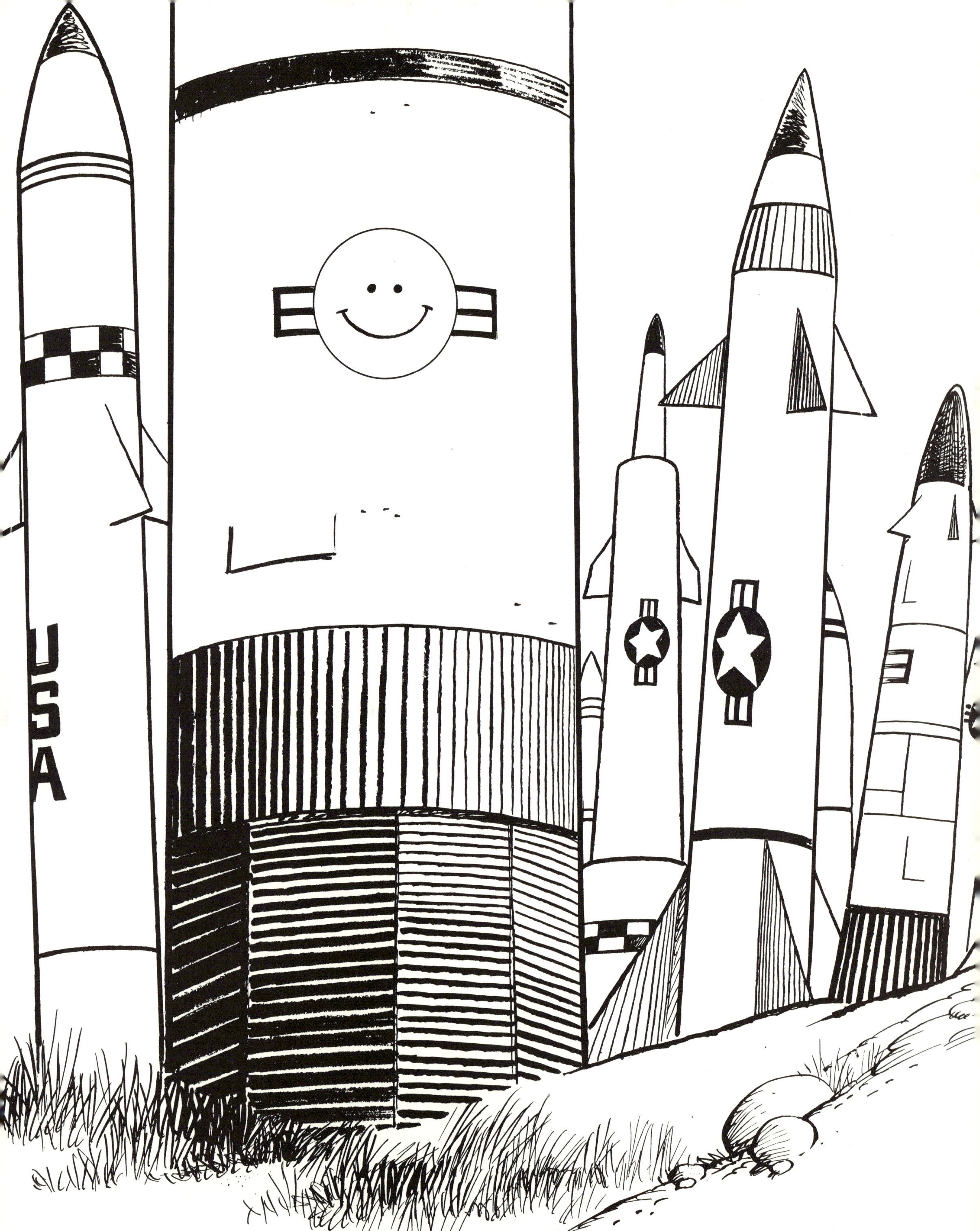
USA

This is our nuclear arsenal.
Color it mushroom gray.
We have enough to destroy the world fifty times over.
Still the Russians have the advantage.
They can destroy the world sixty times over.
Ronnie did not like this.
We increased our capability to seventy times over.
Just to be on the safe side.

OFFICIAL IRAN REPORT

COLORING BOOK

This is the Iran-contra report.
Color it shocking purple with lots of gray areas.
It was one of Ronnie's darkest hours.
He claims he *still* doesn't know what went on.
A nationwide poll was recently taken.
It showed 86 percent of Americans believe Ronnie's story.
This is encouraging except for one thing.
Same poll showed 86 percent believe in flying saucers!

Color these different faces the same.
They are all our Ronnie.
He was an actor before he was president.
Some say he was an actor even *while* he was president.
Ronnie starred in a great many films.
He played a lot of different parts.
But whatever the role, Ronnie's *real* self came through.
He wasn't a very *good* actor!

This is Ronnie a long time ago.
Color him very, very green.
He was a sports announcer on radio.
That's how he started his climb to the top.
He learned early how to play ball.

Here is Ronnie as a TV host.
Color him in early black and white.
It was for the weekly "GE Theatre."
General Electric finally had to let him go.
He *turned off* a lot of people.

Ronnie became head of the screen actors' union.
Color him bold and brassy.
This was a very important job.
He dealt with lots of producers and directors.
Still he couldn't get work as an actor!

GO EAST

This is the state building in California.
When you color it, use lots of oranges.
Ronnie used to govern there.
He was a very good governor.
He solved the unemployment problem in California.
He sent the jobless to Nevada.
He also stopped welfare cheating in the state.
He did away with all the social programs.

THE
PRESIDENT'S
NAP
SCHEDULE

MON... 10 AM
2 PM
TUES... 11 AM
3 PM
WED... 9 AM
1 PM

OVER

My, what a pretty office!
It is a pretty *oval* office.
Color it eggshell.
This is where Ronnie does his work.
It is also where Ronnie takes his nap.
Very often at the same time.
Everyone agrees Ronnie is doing a great job in this office.
Only they wish he were doing it in the *rest* of the country!

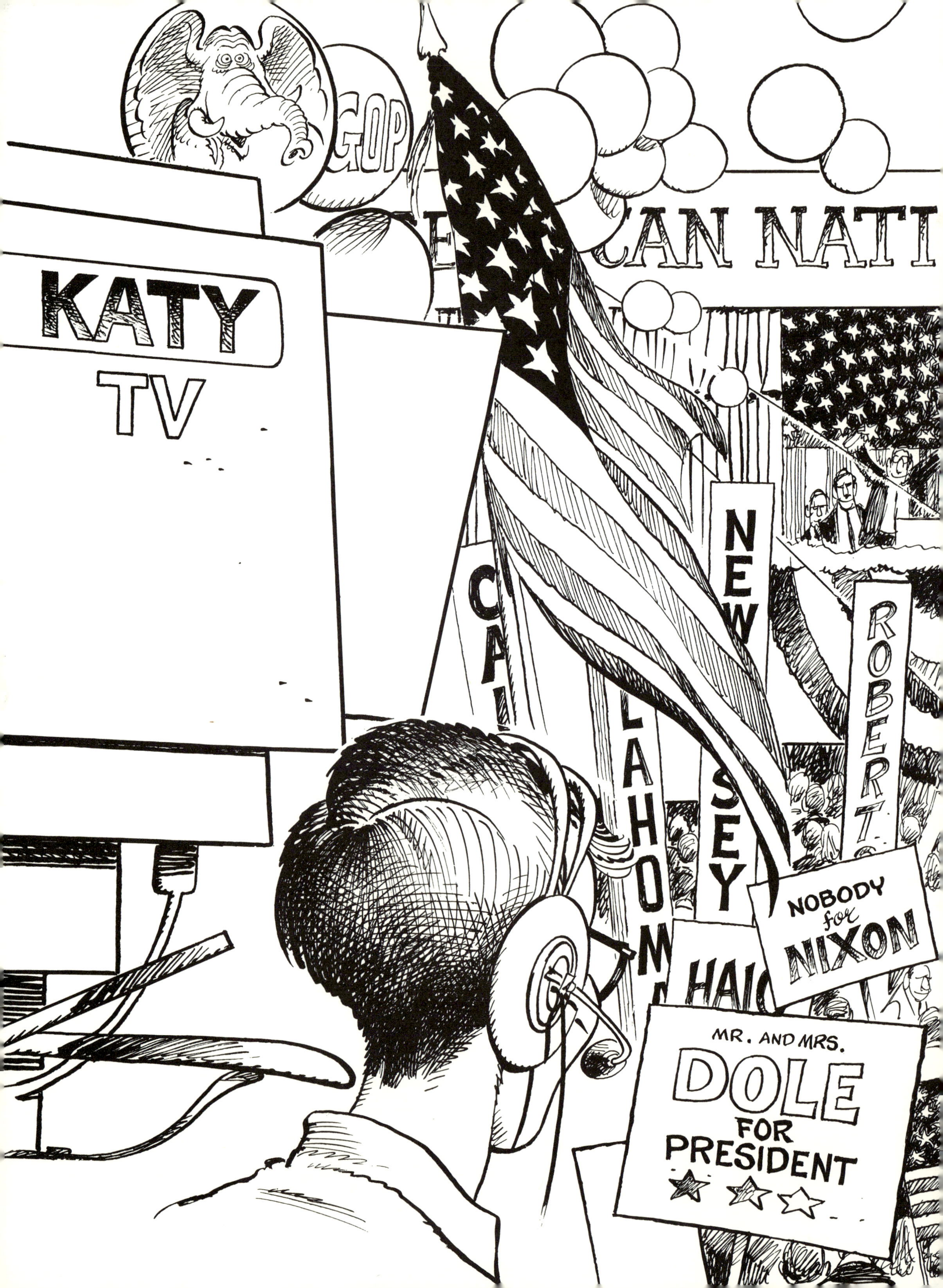

GOP
CAN NATI
KATY
TV
NEW
SEY
LAHOM
ROBERT
NOBODY for NIXON
HAIG
MR. AND MRS.
DOLE
FOR
PRESIDENT

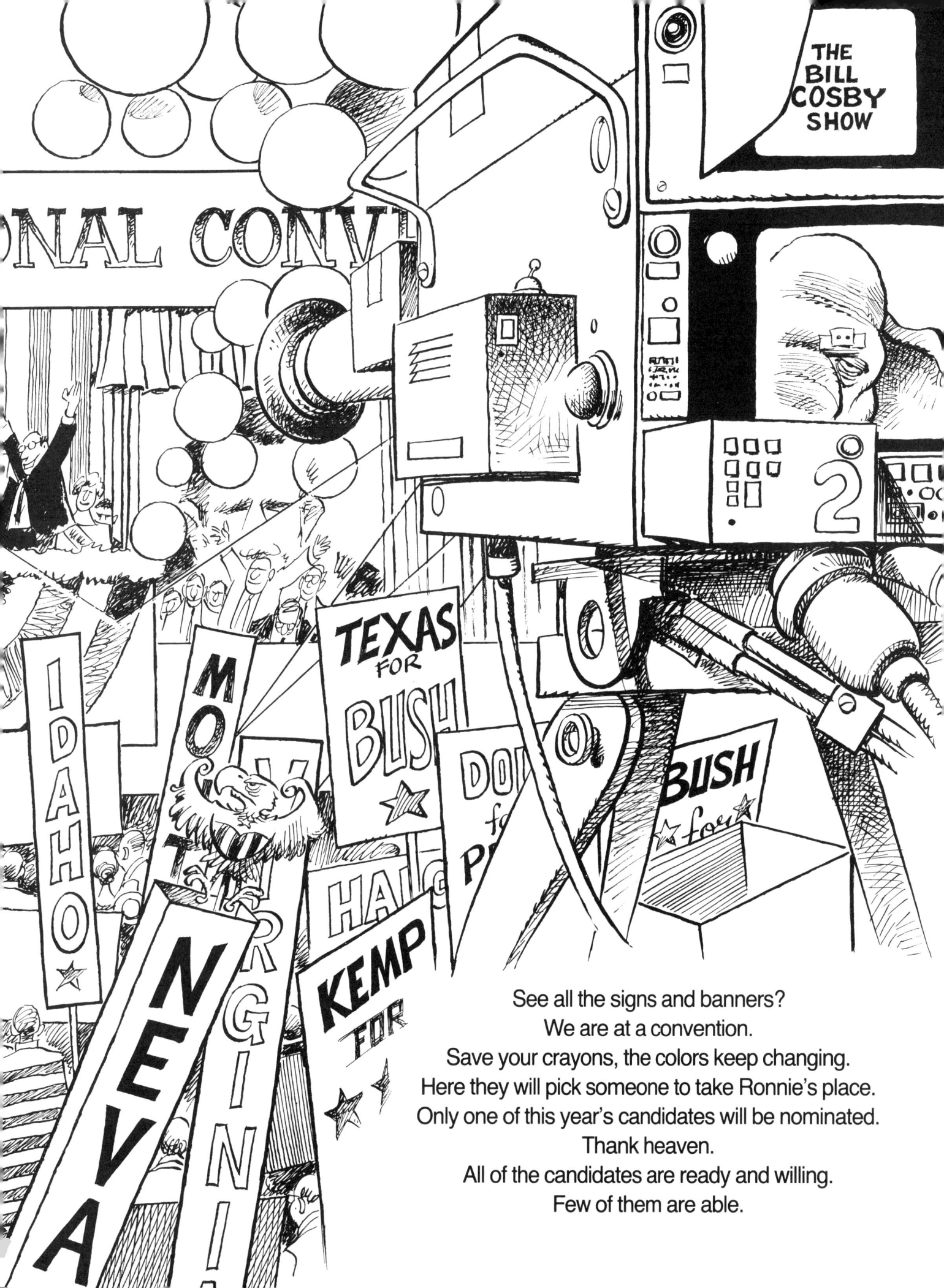

See all the signs and banners?
We are at a convention.
Save your crayons, the colors keep changing.
Here they will pick someone to take Ronnie's place.
Only one of this year's candidates will be nominated.
Thank heaven.
All of the candidates are ready and willing.
Few of them are able.

These men are Ronnie's friends.
They are all conservatives.
Color them true blue.
Many of them are under investigation.
Some of them have even been indicted.
These men have done a lot for this country.
They have taken hanky-panky out of the streets.
They have put it in the White House.

These men are Ronnie's enemies.
They are all liberals.
Color them shrinking violet.
They don't do anything right.
They are ruining the country.
They shouldn't even be in this book.
Why did we include these people here?
We like to be fair to *everybody!*

See the funny little man with Ronnie?
It is Ronnie's new friend, Gorby.
Whatever you do, don't color Gorby's forehead.
It is already colored.
Here they are at a summit meeting.
They have come to sign an important treaty.
No, not a strategic arms cut treaty.
It is a *peace* treaty between Nancy and Mrs. Gorby!

This man is another of Ronnie's friends.
Even if you color him he still looks black and white.
Ronnie always calls on this friend for advice.
This friend advised Ronnie to sell arms to Iran.
He advised him to send the marines into Lebanon.
He advised him to nominate Judge Bork to the Supreme Court.
With friends like this, you don't need friends!

This is Grenada.
Color it soft and serene.
It is the site of Ronnie's big military battle.
He sent in hundreds of paratroopers and marines.
He sent in bazookas and antiaircraft guns.
He sent in tanks and warships and fighter planes.
In three days he totally wiped out the enemy.
All six of them.

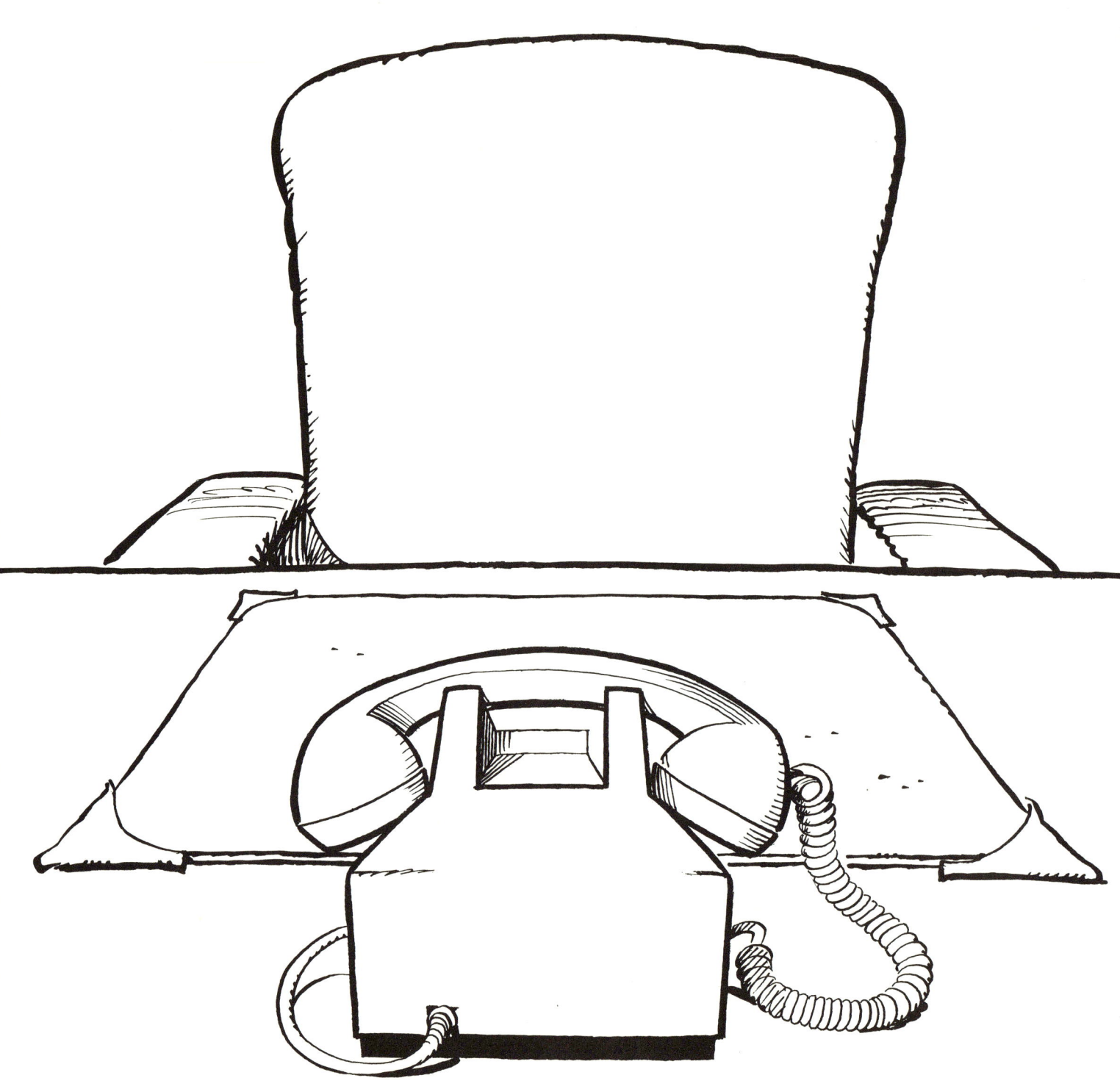

This is a very special telephone.
It is a *Hot Line.*
Don't color it because you shouldn't touch it.
Only two people get to use this telephone.
The two most important people in the world.
It is there only for an emergency.
It hasn't been used for quite some time now.
They're waiting for the phone company to repair it!

See the man feeding the monkey?
Yes, that is our Ronnie.
He is the one on the left.
Color his face blushing red.
Ronnie once acted with a chimpanzee.
He is sorry about that.
It's been the laughingstock of his entire career.
Up until he became president, that is!

Look at what we have here!
It is Ronnie's latest birthday cake.
Do not bother to color the candles.
You probably haven't enough crayons.
Other presidents grow older-looking while in office.
Ronnie looks the same today as when he started.
This is because he lets others do all the work.
With Ronnie, his *cabinet* and *staff* grow older-looking!

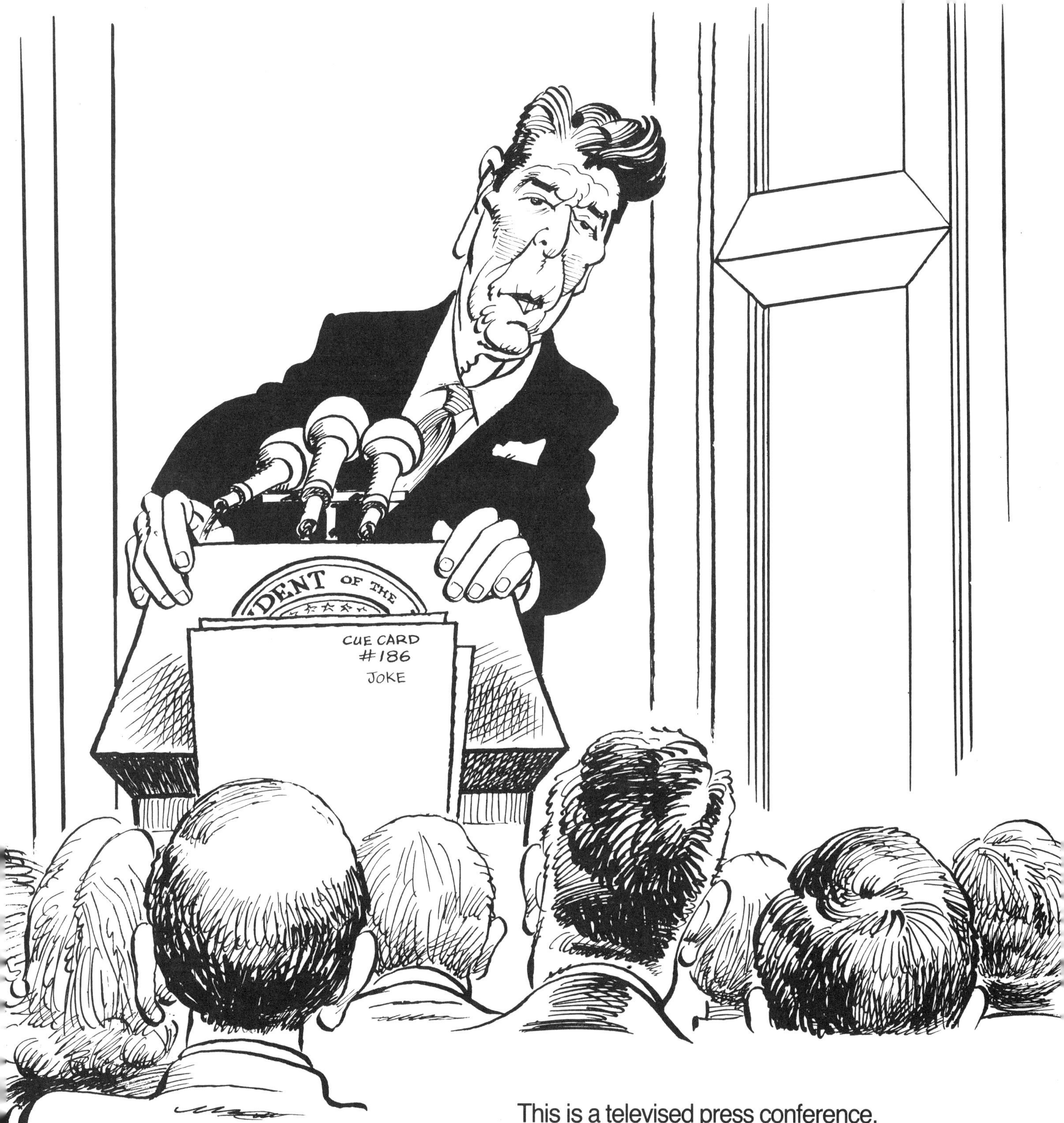

CUE CARD
#186
JOKE

This is a televised press conference.
Color it bright and flashy.
Here they ask Ronnie all kinds of questions.
Ronnie gives them all kinds of answers.
Sometimes they are the answers to the questions.
No matter what they ask, Ronnie is ready.
He knows all the answers.
He is reading from cue cards.

This is Ronnie's latest *budget.*
Color it bone white.
See how lopsided it is?
Ronnie plans to even it all out.
He will eliminate the social spending.
They say Ronnie doesn't like poor people.
This is just not true.
Look how many he's created in the last eight years!

military
spending

social
spending

DEFICIT

This is Ronnie's latest *deficit.*
Color it out of sight.
People complain he hasn't done anything about the deficit.
Ronnie says this isn't so.
He reduced it right after the stock market crash.
Before the crash, the deficit was a trillion dollars.
He reduced it to a hundred million billion dollars!
This is called Reaganomics.

Time now for a look at history's great leaders.
Sitting Bull rallied all the Indian tribes to military victory.
Color him red.
Mahatma Gandhi won independence for the entire Indian nation.
Color him brown.
Mao Tse-tung united one billion people into a powerful China.
Color him yellow.
As for Ronnie—color him *pale* by comparison!

Hello, what have we here?
It is a defense system in outer space.
It is Star Wars.
Color it dark and foreboding.
Many people say it will not work.
Ronnie says it will.
Ronnie says he is *sure* it will work.
He saw it in a movie once.

This is the Supreme Court.
Use only conservative colors here.
See how it is tilting to the right?
Ronnie has made it that way.
This court could return us to where we once were.
This court could restore us to our former innocence.
This court could bring us back to our pioneer spirit.
This court could set us back a hundred years!

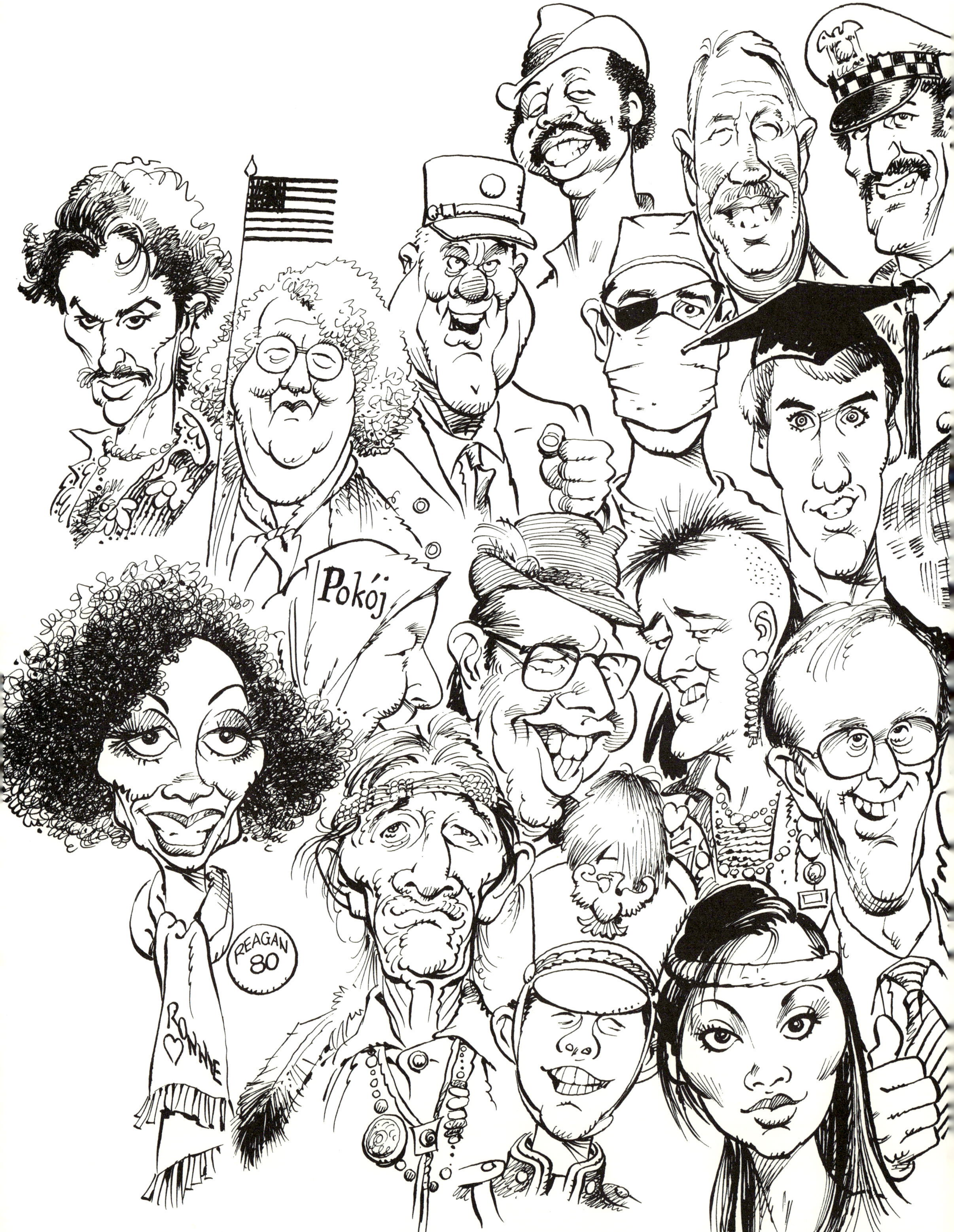
Pokój
REAGAN 80
RONNIE

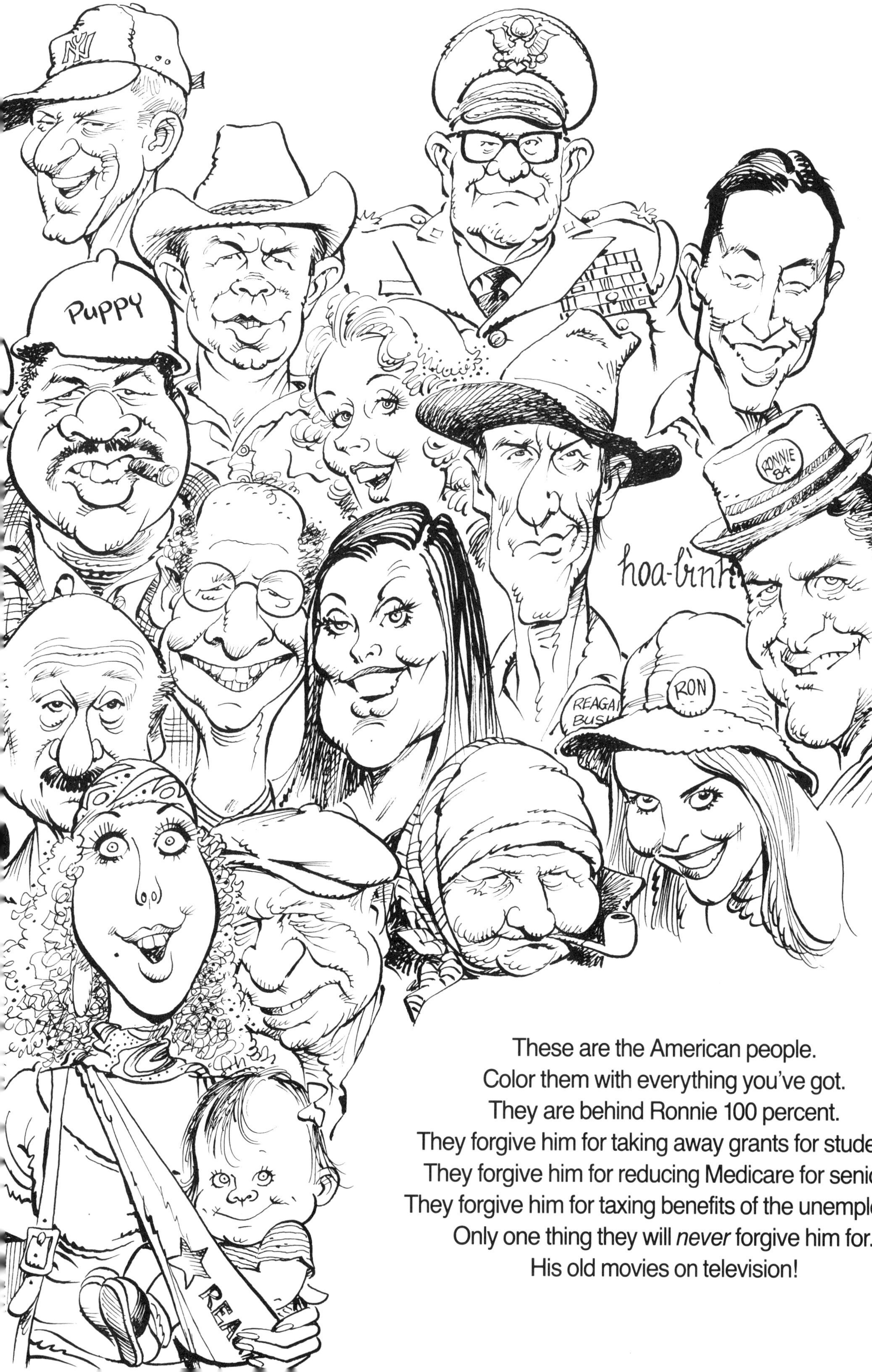
PUPPY
hoa-binh
RONNIE 84
RON
REAGA BUS
REA

These are the American people.
Color them with everything you've got.
They are behind Ronnie 100 percent.
They forgive him for taking away grants for students.
They forgive him for reducing Medicare for seniors.
They forgive him for taxing benefits of the unemployed.
Only one thing they will *never* forgive him for.
His old movies on television!

Wave goodbye to Ronnie.
He is riding off into the sunset.
It is not a movie, it is real life.
Use your fade-out colors here.
We will all miss our dear old Ronnie.
We have a lot to be thankful for.
Things won't be the same in this country without him.
That's the *main* thing we have to be thankful for!